PAUSING FOR
PARENTAL PERUSAL

*A collection of articles dealing with the well-being,
Happiness and success of children/students*

Margaret Redfern

authorHOUSE®

AuthorHouse™
1663 Liberty Drive
Bloomington, IN 47403
www.authorhouse.com
Phone: 1 (800) 839-8640

Published by AuthorHouse   04/04/2016

ISBN: 978-1-5049-3270-7 (sc)
ISBN: 978-1-5049-3269-1 (e)

Library of Congress Control Number: 2015913510

Print information available on the last page.

This book is printed on acid-free paper.

Table of Contents

Dedication

I dedicate the contents of this book in loving memory of my dear friend Elizabeth Marie Watton, who listened to every word in every chapter as it was written. She lived out her own dedicated teaching career in guiding her special needs students to recognize that they were special to her and therefore very special within themselves.

I also recognize within the contents of the articles those whose lives are intricately woven within the life patterns of children/students within their care, parents, teachers, caretakers, guardians, and other involved adults.

I invite the readers to peruse the following published articles, all dealing with the well-being, happiness, and success of children/students. Perhaps we can focus on each value as the accompanied stressed message within each article's concept. Come read with me!

The following articles appeared in the *Melrose Free Press*, the *Malden Observer,* and the *Malden Magazine*.

Professional Endorsements

Miss Redfern's love and compassion for family and children will never end. After teaching for so many years, we might think her retirement would be a good-bye, but it's not; instead she continues to guide parents with her great ideas. As a mother, I never realized there was a difference when you say to a child, "You can do it" and "I believe you can do it." In Miss Redfern's book, I learned that when you say, "I believe you can do it," that makes a huge difference. It gives the child a much stronger desire to try things, and after they accomplish whatever they were trying to do, they feel so happy and make the parent feel proud too. I want to say thank you to Miss Redfern.

Ydalgade Alceus, certified nursing assistant

In *Pausing for Parental Perusal*, Margaret Redfern models ways of looking at children with love, compassion, and respect for the freedom and rights of the child by sharing with the reader many wisdom-packed stories unique to her years of teaching young children. Her nurturing ways of carefully opening the gift of the child to the child's unique individual gifts helps the child to experience joy and appreciation in learning and growing and love and respect for her/himself and others. This book is a great resource not only for parents, teachers, and substitute teachers but for anyone who cares for children or about children.

Don't let the title, *Pausing for Parental Perusal,* mislead you into thinking that this book is only for parents. I especially recommend this book to anyone who was born into a family structure without nurture. Redfern shows how to put into action love, respect, and compassion for the parent and child in all of us. Indeed, it is a powerful work of hope and joy.

Susan A. Rotondi, MA, pastoral minister, spiritual director

Writing with straight honesty and deepest sincerity, Margaret Redfern speaks with a message that is simple and satisfying, yet dynamic and challenging. Even if you think you have heard it all before, this book will enable you to look at the biggest questions on parenting and education.

It is my opinion that this book is dedicated to everyone who works with children. I have no doubt it will be used as a teaching tool on every level of education.

Maureen Tighe, former principal, Malden Public School, Massachusetts

I feel this book has many simple, down-to-earth truths that can benefit not only parents but also teachers, coaches, and anyone else who values and interacts with children.

Patricia Faro, school psychologist, Massachusetts

Finally! An honest-to-goodness user-friendly book for parents, grandparents, and all caregivers of children. It's full of good and truly useful parenting tips that are easy to follow and don't require any fancy ingredients. And best of all? They work!

Please accept my thoughts about Margaret Redfern's book.

Deb Walsh, Melrose, Massachusetts, mother of three boys, ages seventeen, fifteen, and thirteen

Don't let the title, *Pausing for Parental Perusal*, fool you for a second. The wisdom within these pages is priceless. I wish I had had this book when my first daughter was born. I believe it would have made a world of difference in the way I parented my children. The approach with which Margaret Redfern grabs your attention within the pages of her short stories is from the child within each of us. I felt, in reading the stories, the author knew me and my inner child who went unnoticed. *Pausing for Parental Perusal* is a great read for anyone who wants or needs to know how to relate and be heard in dealing with people, be they children or adults.

Nancy McInerney, mother of three girls, personal trainer, Medford, Massachusetts

After forty years of teaching in regular grades and the last twenty years with special needs young children ages six to nine, I came across Miss Redfern's beautifully written treatise. This is no ordinary book on the dos and don'ts of parenthood. It is inspirational guidance focusing on the part we cannot see within our children/students as is introduced in her opening chapter, "Inside vs. Outside." She tells us that we must guide our children/students from the inside out, not for what they do but for who they are while making challenging choices within their lives from preschool to college levels. She cautions us that choices do form futures. And isn't that the truth! This book will bring blessings to parents and to all who enter children's lives.

Elizabeth Watton

Former Teacher

Preface

Reading, writing, 'rithmetic! For eons of time, these skills have been the rite of passage to happiness and success within our children/students. They contain a program of knowledge, techniques, strategies, etc., that lead to a well-earned paycheck in their lives.

However, when we so heavily stress and demand success, children/students can fall between the cracks within their own individualities. With so much emphasis on parental and scholastic achievement, the acknowledgment of the inside is often overlooked. Children are so often judged on what they do or what they fail to do that the more important focus on who they are is often lost.

As you read the introduction at the beginning of this book, you will be presented with the depths of my beliefs through having shared one hundred eighty days for forty years with approximately fourteen hundred students. The "Introduction" and "Inside vs. Outside" say it all!

I invite you to read on!

—Margaret Redfern, Author

Introduction

"Why Don't Our Flowers Blossom?" reminds us of the reassurance our children need within a negative or harmful experience that they are not what they do. Their personhoods are separate from their deeds. Our children need to be nurtured from the inside out.

"Nurturing" focuses on the concept that our children need to be recognized for who they are within the parts of them we as parents cannot see. In the gardens of their early childhoods are the roots of preteens, teenagers, and college students, which need our attention more often and more deeply than the instant gratification of the outer marketing world.

The application is designed to take ten minutes, with specific sharings being offered.

"Heroism vs. Violence" is where we meet Ed, a high school hero to his peers and unknowingly a fictional hero to himself. With the help of a course on heroism/violence within his curriculum, Ed meets Jiminy Cricket, who leads Ed's inner self, the part others cannot see, to become aware of the true concept of heroism.

"Courage" is the value accompaniment of this article. Courage is involved within the parts we cannot see in our children. True heroism focuses on making the challenging choice to do the right thing and make the healthy decision, which involves deep courage. The application is an invitation to share concepts of violence and heroism.

"A Propositional Preposition" states the preposition *with* must replace *to* and *at* in sharing reading times as well as other times with our children. The article leads to the lesson found between the lines as it is absorbed within the parts we cannot see.

"Acceptance" is the value that highlights the lesson within this article. It springs from the intrinsic yearning to be recognized and acknowledged as a valued being within the respective personhood of every child at every age. The application is specific offerings while reading with the child.

"Stop, Thief!" Here we meet Jake, the despondent owner of a service station that was broken into. He finds things that are valuable to him have been stolen. Jake discovers the lock on his garage door failed to secure his valued possessions. He also realizes life has become too busy for him to take the time to add stronger safety measures to protect what he loves.

"Values" is the focusing point of this article, which presents awareness of the lure of protecting material possessions versus the nurturing of values within the personhood of each child.

The application is listings per grade levels of specific questions about nurturing inner values we shared with our children/family.

"To Be or Not to Be" speaks directly to the core issues already mentioned. "To Be" stresses the concept of life shown by positive, healthy choices. "Not to Be" implies a state of chaos and tragedy as the result of negative behavior through harmful choices.

"Choices" follows this article and reminds children of all ages that happiness and success depend on the kinds of choices they will make.

The application is specific comments of "To Be" choices in attaining happiness and self-belief or "Not to Be" choices, leading to tragedy or failure.

"A Marketing Strategy—Polishing the Product" restates the premise that the new car, the camera, the cell phone, the wardrobe, the hairstyle, and so on are shiny, bright articles that bring excitement into lives. Its message can refer back to within the article as it may pose the questions, "Why don't …" or perhaps, "Why won't our children blossom?" since the polishing is only done on the outside.

"Affirmation" is the accompanying value of the efforts made by children of all ages to be polished on the inside, the emotional system, the part we cannot see. They seek affirmative polish not for what they have or have not done but more importantly, for who they are.

The application in suggested topics, include an exchange of child's/student's world with parental insights into that world.

"Fitting Together the Pieces of the Academic Pie" shares how the concepts and arrival of the MA MCAS testing system came as a shock to the three constituents of the educational systems throughout the state of Massachusetts. Parents, teachers, and students are echoed, not unlike the shot heard round the world. Actually, it served the same purpose; it was a rallying cry to wake up and recognize the urgency of preparing our students to protect their own sovereign rights to happiness and success.

"Education" as a completely defined value addresses the academic pie of this article. It reminds us that the first wedge of pie is cut from the academic world of preschool and forms roots through elementary years, culminating between middle school and high school academics. It suggests that we cannot expect students to be served the entire pie all at once at the high school level and produce a successful outcome. There must be continued involvement throughout the earlier years toward graduation achievement.

The application is to make a daily effort to express belief and pride in the efforts made by children/students at all grade levels.

"Final Focus" is a personal offering from the author about respecting the efforts of parents/adults as they face the daily challenges within the part they cannot see within those they serve and their lives' journeys.

What's Inside the Wrapper?

Happy birthday! This greeting is excitedly absorbed by birthday celebrants beginning around the second half of their first decades and extending into the teen years. Which way are children's eyes riveted as guests arrive—in an upward glance at the smiling faces or in an inquisitive expectancy straight ahead, at a gift whose mystery will soon be exposed? The freedom of childhood allows the gift to be important and is also an acceptable reaction by those sharing in this gala event.

This scene is often reenacted during holidays and other festive occasions. Adults witness excited hands pulling off ribbons and bows, totally stripping the package of glittering wrappers to hastily discover the mystery of its contents.

In view of the growing awareness and concerns over the well-being of our children in today's world of various challenges, is there a lesson here for us in reviewing these eventful times?

Stop for a moment. We must think of our children, bring them to our mind's eye, and ask ourselves, "What's inside this wrapper?" Very often, like a gift, we take for granted what we see on the outside. Our conclusion is often a stereotyped vision that remains static through the years. The package is a child predisposed to our care and guidance, with responsibility on his or her part to honor and obey our tenets—homework, chores, being ready to go where and when we need to go, listening to and performing do's and don'ts.

However, we need to apply this question differently than when asking about a boxed present. The time has come to ask ourselves, "What's inside the wrapper of my child?" My concerns for our children have brought me to the realization we do take care of our children's needs. We feed, clothe, and shelter them. We drive them to various destinations. All of this is taking care of the outside of the child. It is the inside that must deal with daily challenges and decisions.

If our children continue to live robot-like lives with our minds in their heads, why do we expect them to make valuable judgments and choices if that preparation has not been nurtured? The "I-ness" of our children has become a "we-ness." The body simply complies with our directions, and that is what our stereotyped vision dictates to us. We need to understand that just as crawling and gradual standing allow a baby's legs to attain the strength to walk, so the nurturing of the child's mind will strengthen the child in making choices leading to a belief in himself or herself. We need to become aware of the underlying value of giving strength to this inner need. We need to ask our children's opinions in everyday situations, thus strengthening those intangible assets that reinforce a self-belief. This belief stems from finding value within based on a decision or judgment others respect. It is founded on who they are and not on what they do. Unfortunately, many children feel they are what they do because adults may unintentionally react this way.

I witnessed a scene between a parent and child of about four years of age as they came from a nearby restaurant. The child was overwhelmed and in tears that seemed to come from the very depth of her being. The parent's angry, accusing words were, "You bad, bad girl."

Questioning this whole puzzling episode, the child's younger brother asked, "Mommy, what did she do?"

The parent exasperatedly replied, "Didn't you see how she played with the silverware?"

Recalling the parent's judgmental words, my heart wondered how the child could handle such a destructive comment. Indeed, a seed was sown that the child would painfully review in the future. In my opinion, the parent's comments were prompted by an adult's expectations and addressed to another adult in the guise of a child. The parent seemingly has unrealistic expectations of a small child's ability to display the finesse of an adult's standard for table manners. However, a small child's brain is not yet developed to the point of making a distinction between unacceptable and acceptable behaviors. A child tends to think, *I am what I do.*

Children often see themselves as a result of an adult's judgment of them. We witness and remember good times, the happy smiles when receiving affirmation of a job well done. We sometimes seem to be unaware of the presence of rejection when we penetrate the same inner space with a negative reaction, which turns affirmation into self-blame.

Another interesting incidence is observed as the children leave the school building at the end of school. The younger ones are often greeted with smiles, questions, and comments such as, "What did you do in school today?" "Oh, what a nice paper you did." "Tell me about that pretty drawing." "I'm proud of that sticker on your paper." As older, middle-grade children appear, the comments often change: "Did you pass the test?" "What homework do you have?" "Hurry up and get in the car." "We have to go shopping." "Get your homework done before baseball practice." I often heard these comments as I dismissed my classes.

What is happening here? Does becoming an eight-, nine-, or ten-year-old preclude affirmation? As children get older, do they need less nurturing? Do they deserve to have less interest and involvement shown to their world of school? Since they understand our adult conversations with them, does it mean they need our love and attention less? We need to greet and share an honest interest toward the world of our school children at all grade levels and allow this affirmation into the inside of the package, going beyond the physical form of the outside of the package as it emerges from a day at school.

Found inside the human wrapper are countless gifts to be recognized and allowed to be shared. We need to offer our children the opportunity to present their opinions from a belief system within themselves. "What do you think about what we shared earlier?" "How do you feel about …" "Let's both share our thoughts about …"

Giving them these opportunities plants the seed within them that their values are valued, and so are they. These responses are not based on what they have done but flow from an inner belief of who they are. These beliefs are strengthened year by year, and our children become prepared to stand on their own inner trust. A "Thank you for your thoughts" from adults would help seal this affirmation. The "we-ness" of parent and child needs to be slowly and reassuringly become nurtured in the "I-ness" within them within the early childhood years into the world of the teenager.

A daily sharing in and receiving of what our children offer is nurturing them through their own inner giving, resulting in positive growth patterns. Thus, inside the wrapper of the child's personhood will be an established affirmation that he or she is a valuable asset to life among his or her peers.

Note Page

From the third paragraph, can you answer the question, "What's inside the wrapper of my child?"

Jot down your thoughts on this note page.

Choose one of the paragraphs in this chapter, and write about which one has the deepest meaning to you.

Share your reasons on this note page.

Outside vs Inside

Outside
Cars, Clothes, Cell Phones

Inside
Roots, Affirmations, Choices

Outside vs. Inside

We always care for the outside of the body. The five senses are parts of the outside of our bodies.

The eyes are healed with drops or surgery, and vision is corrected with glasses. There are hearing aids to help us hear well. We get sensory warnings from our olfactory nerves, causing us to turn away from dangerous or discomforting odors. Touching objects that produce pain activates our autonomic nervous system, and we pull our hands or feet away from the source of possible damage to our sense of touch. Our taste buds almost instantly alert us of a disturbing sample of food or drink, and we reject this sample by drinking it or swallowing it, followed by a drink of water or juice and often accompanied by a prayer.

The mystery or challenge remains as to what corresponding care and nurturing we can offer to our children/students, unlike that of the senses to the part we cannot see. I believe this unseen part of humans is the cornerstone upon which happiness and success must be built by children within themselves. So often our focus is on the outer evidence of success—the mark on the paper, the homework to be done, the project to be completed. I believe we must continue to make a gallant effort to reach the inside, the place or space within our children where the affirmation of them as people will forever need nurturing, most especially within their academic journey.

Note Page

From within your parental role, have you ever read such a comparison being made between the outside and the inside needs of your children as found in this chapter? Write your answer on this note page.

As read in the third line of the last paragraph of this chapter, have you been able to share in the unseen part within your child?

Thank you, and please continue with your reading.

Why Don't Our Flowers Blossom?

Outside
Peer Pressure, Complacency, Exclusion

Inside
Nurturing
Time, Sharing, Acknowledgment

Why Don't Our Flowers Blossom?

The last of the wintry blasts had retreated. The car had been cleared of its burden of white snow and its windows scraped clean of frost. It was late March, and the expectancy of spring growth was just around the corner. It was time to replace white, six-sided snowflakes with the hope that arrives simultaneously with new shoots pushing through fresh earth. It was time to envision the joy that my senses would revel in as I mentally previewed the blossoms that would bring me so much pleasure.

An old cliché came to my mind that reminded me that beauty does not arrive under its own power: "You don't get something for nothing." The only way my flowers would give me the gift of beauty and satisfaction would be if I gave them the proper tending on a daily basis once the seeds had been planted in the earth. The earth itself held its natural supply of protection within the soil. My job was to nurture them with food, water, sunshine, shade, a sturdy stick if necessary, and other outer elements that foster growth. These gardening procedures would indeed reward me with a beautiful array of blossoms, and the flowers themselves would enjoy the surrounding setting of the garden.

Like a favorite verse of childhood, "I watched my garden grow," tending to the outer needs with a feeling of having furnished all my plants would need to grow into healthy blossoms. I watched and waited, only to see the stem that supports the blossom begin to weaken, the outer petals gently drop off, tiny brown specks appear on the new growth, and a fresh, new bud wither rather than bloom. The plants that had inwardly had a chance to blossom into a life of their own had lost that opportunity.

As I was soon to perceive, in my haste to tend to the stem, the leaves, the petals, and the buds, I unknowingly neglected the roots, the unseen source of strength. The roots are the parts with many threads that spread into the surrounding areas of space where they were planted. In an effort to explain the absence of my expected array of blossoms, I realized that I had not remembered this one part of the plant that makes it into an individual flower it is to become, unlike other flowers in the garden. It is the part that gives it its own identity—the *root*. I didn't remember to tend the root that would prevent it from stunting its growth or destroying the essence of its being.

As I muse over this lesson in flower blossoming, I am reminded of other living beings, many of which do not blossom into their full potential, like my flowers. It seems to me that the pattern is similar. The child is born or planted into a family unit. In the first few years, the earth around it is tended so carefully with, "I love you," hugs, cuddling, smiles, being read to, examining pictures in books, feeding times, nap times, etc. The stem begins to grow, the petals form, the buds appear, and a sturdy, young child appears before us. Soon it is time for the roots to begin to discover inner trails of challenges, and the undaunted child follows this spirit of growth from its inside down within the soil from which it was given its life.

However, as its young life continues, this living being begins to feel the effect of less time spent being nurtured as other responsibilities appear in the daily life cycle of the caregiver. Just as with my flower garden, my time began to be consumed with other necessary concerns in my life, yet I expected my flowers to grow and give me joy in their blossoming. The one all-important factor I had misplaced into other concerns and displaced from my garden was *time* spent among the flowers in spraying, pruning, loosening the soil, but nonetheless, *time* spent with what was most precious to my happiness would have given the fullest inner growth possible to the loving things in my care.

In the garden of human beings, there is no difference between the deep need for *time* spent with them during these years when their roots are following the beckoning of unknown challenges. I believe we desperately need to acknowledge that the age levels of plants and children make little difference in the amount of *time* we offer to spend with them in all stages of their lives. It only took me ten minutes to water my plants—the same amount of time to read one small paragraph and hear what it means to each other. It would take another ten minutes of another day telling what each other did at a specific time. Another day another ten minutes would be spent telling each other of a choice made that day and the consequences of that choice. Another day, another ten minutes, exchanging experiences and finding reason to say, "I'm proud of you." And the ten-minute daily list goes on.

Can you visualize these inner roots? In those ten-minute stretches of *time*, those roots are discovering ways to emerge from the earth with stronger, fibrous roots of affirmation. I believe the flowering within so many of our children does not blossom into our hopeful expectations because those traveling, self-seeking roots are kept beneath the earth unwatered by adult acknowledgments and therefore dry up and become gnarled within themselves and never blossom. Often, like the plant, more expensive treatment like a consultant is called in. Also, like the plant, it is long and hard work to uncover and unsnarl roots that have become warped and tightly wound around themselves.

I found it necessary to be aware that the older plants in my garden also need the same ten-minute doses of nurturing. Older plants tend to fool us by making us think they are okay because they look okay. In older children we can be fooled into thinking they are okay because they resemble us as adults. On the contrary, this often is the exact time when what appears to becoming a promising bud breaks off the stem because the dosage of *time* has been lessened. Actually, during these preteen to teen years I highly recommend upping the dosage wherever and whenever possible. The roots will become inwardly strengthened, the stems will reach upward into the sky, and the tightly closed buds will be more prone to burst into a happy self-identified flower. In return, the caregiver, the gardener, will have that hopeful expectancy realized. *Happy gardening!*

Focusing
Nurturing

The term I would use to indicate the depth of the message in this article, as already stressed, is *root*. Growing, rearing, and guiding, whether in reference to flowers or children, all have a common denominator. Each new growth, whether via a seed or human birth, begins its own growth when roots begin to sprout. The plant is taken from the rooting water, and its tendrils of new life are gently placed within healthy soil to be nourished for its own direction. The human seed has been nourished within the pod of the womb, and like the plant seed, the newly formed and nourished embryo makes its need for its new home known. It is replanted into the arms of its parent(s). From this moment on, in both cases, plant and human, the caretaker must never lose sight of the *roots* of this new, living growth.

As with the plant, the obvious dependency of the infant for the constant, continued attention to its various needs is quickly forthcoming. Its physical needs of food, sleep, bathing, etc., are tended to on a timely schedule, as well as hugs, kisses, and caresses. Also, just as with a plant, various distractions in our day cause us to forget to water and feed it, the same lessening of care often happens to the roots of children, most especially beyond the years of infancy and early childhood. Their dependency on the caretaking is less obvious as they begin to tend to their own physical needs of eating, bathing, playing, etc. Their ability to have intelligent conversations with us lures us away from the earlier pattern of acknowledging their presence and need for recognition. This need for such affirmation is found with the rooted emotional tendril making its way within its own existence but without the same level of awareness of needed nurturing from the caregiver/parent.

Most unfortunately, in today's society, television, videos, tapes, movies, lyrics, and headphones are challenging methods of feeding the attention of our children. What used to be an expected segment of the world of the teenager now infiltrates the world of the most vulnerable ages of eight years and into elementary schools. The length of time spent viewing movies or playing video games can be controlled. However, we cannot control the mental image that may have been imprinted within the memory of our children. Neither can we control the silent choices dictated by such viewings within the challenges met by these young people and often made with no parental awareness that such thoughts exist within our children.

Indeed, many of our children do blossom. I believe the strongest link to this evolvement of children into happiness within their lives can be traced back to the awareness and acknowledgment to the emotional *root* being nurtured throughout infancy and early childhood but most urgently throughout the preteen and teenage years.

Let us take a clue from our physical systems. When the taste buds and stomach receive nourishing and pleasing food, the body lives each day in a healthy physical condition. Once more, let us not forget the emotional system or *root* being part of the whole person/child/student. Time spent together will indeed foster a blossoming into a happy, successful, and self-reliant being.

Note Page

What reaction did the last paragraph of this chapter cause within you as a parent? Do you identify with the last line in that paragraph? You may write your thoughts below on this note page.

How important to you is awareness, as conveyed in the last paragraph of the "Focusing" section?

Continue writing on this note page. Thank you for your thoughts. Continue with your reading.

Heroism vs. Violence

Ed's anger had been heating up all week. He could feel it seething through his nervous system as he awoke in the morning. He had to return to school, where he again would see his former girlfriend chatting coquettishly with other male students. Total disbelief would grip him as he struggled to figure out why she had rejected him, not recognizing his obvious qualities and heroic gestures as she had once done. He had become the central figure in the schoolyard huddle who dared to show the others that it was "cool" to take a puff from a drug-laden butt. He was the "hero" when he would be the one to challenge another student to settle an argument after school and off of school grounds. A vacuum had been created by the absence of somebody, anybody, who would accept him as he was, as well as the silent, tantalizing inner wish that he was needed somewhere by someone in his life.

His thoughts seemed to be cemented in his mind as he mulled over everyday occurrences. Life had become such a fast-paced existence that there seemed no available time to share his thoughts and feelings about issues that were important to him. This isolation prompted him to display misguided heroism in displays of violence at different levels. His honest appraisal of his actions remained in emotional denial. His spirit was being nurtured by the recognition of his peers as they responded to his actions with smiles, applause, and invitations to join the group. Something assured him from within, "it works," "you're noticed," "you are a hero," and "you dare to challenge others."

As he arrived at school that day, he was unaware that his path to possible or perhaps probable perdition would veer off its course. He stopped in the hallway by the bulletin board to read an announcement, the title of which had caught his eye: "Heroism vs. Violence." A fleeting inner acknowledgment of where he was within himself hit him. He continued to read the course description. "This course will offer insights into the nature of heroism as well as violence. At the completion of the course, participants will be required to submit an essay in answer to the following question: "Is violence a valid display of heroism?"

Ed actually found himself wondering if he should attend the course. Would its offerings soothe the nagging unsettlement in his mind as to how he had been acting? Hadn't his different levels of violent behavior validated his status as a hero in the eyes of his peers and most especially in the eyes of his girlfriend?

Like Jiminy Cricket was to Pinocchio, a little voice within him urged him to register and attend the course. When he arrived, the speaker's voice was not overly authoritative or threatening to his ego. He found himself somewhat agreeing with the concepts that were authentically being presented.

The speaker said, "Let us begin by defining our terms as found in an indisputable reference, the dictionary. An argument can lose its validity if it is based on a personal interpretation of a term rather than the stated factual meaning."

"A hero is anyone regarded as having displayed great courage or exceptionally noble or manly qualities or has done a deed or deeds showing him to express such qualities.[1] Violence means violent or unjust exercise of power, injury, outrage."[2]

"Having stated the legitimate meanings of our subjects, we now need to look at and acknowledge the parts that make up the whole of these terms. In the context of heroism, we find mention of noble or manly. Noble means exalted in character or quality; excellent; worthy.[3] In regard to violence we find unjust, not legitimate, fair or just; wrongful. Unrighteous; acting contrary to right or just; wrongful."[4]

As he listened to the presenter's words, Ed involuntarily found that his conscience had the upper hand. There was Jiminy Cricket again, pushing honesty through the self-defensive wall of denial within Ed's mind. He remembered a recently excitable challenge that had been offered to him just yesterday. Feeling his bravado image, he had agreed to share the evening with other macho friends and spray paint graffiti on cars and buildings in the nearby area. However, Jiminy was doing a good job of challenging him to find a balance between graffiti and heroism. Until now, Ed believed his actions would continue to indicate to others that he was heroic in his decision to be daring to confront danger.

But that one word, *noble*, suddenly became a stumbling block to his fun-filled evening. Graffiti, roughly pushing others, fighting, offering cigarettes, etc., were not and now could not be classified as noble—at least not according to Jiminy Cricket! There could be no evidence of being exalted in character in such unpraiseworthy conduct. In fact, the meanings of violence fit snugly around each of the choices he had been recently making in his life. Indeed, he had been unjustly exercising a power within himself, which he saw now undoubtedly had been misguided. In each of the recent issues in dealing with others, he had caused injury and outrage. He could almost visualize Jiminy's eyes staring right into his ego as his recognition of his unrighteous actions was being judged.

Could it be possible that choosing *not* to be involved in these wrongdoings could be the truer acts of heroism? In honesty, a choice needed to be made to a hero to others—to *himself*! Yes, indeed, to say *no* within himself to the "it's only beer," invitation, wearing the logo of explicit violent scenes, hustling the drug-laced butt, or attending ecstasy parties, would unmistakably bespeak the courage of a hero.

As Ed continued sitting in the class, it was amazing that for the last five or ten minutes he hadn't heard a word the presenter had been offering. Jiminy Cricket and himself had been exchanging a more honest and meaningful conversation. As painful as it was to accept and truthfully realize, he could choose to replace violence with noble acts. In doing so, perhaps his girlfriend would recognize his efforts and once again choose to spend quality time with her newly classified hero.

---

[1] *Funk & Wagnall's Standard Dictionary*, 1966.

[2] Ibid.

[3] Ibid.

[4] Ibid.

Suddenly, Ed remembered the required assignment for concluding the class. He was now ready and willing to submit a well-formulated essay and firmly state his personal belief that violence is not and never will be a valid display of heroism.

The final objective of the presenter was an invitation to those adults who had listened to his offered insights to review the concepts of the lecture with their children/students as an avenue of shared conversational opinions. This columnist also offers the above invitation!

Focusing
Courage

It seems to me that the focusing term in "Heroism vs. Violence" is *courage*. I believe there is an indisputable formula for courage. *Honesty plus self-belief equals courage.* Honesty is inextricably connected to a value of some dimension of acknowledgment within us. Honesty cannot be exclusively allied to lying versus truth. Honesty has a depth to its application within our lives. Stark naked honesty is a deeper and further intrusion into the nature of this most worthy value.

Ed, as we meet him in the article, has been living in the realm of denial, the opposing foe of honesty. His misguided heroism in his display of violence was fueling an invalid conception of himself as a daring figure. Hence, his position in respect to his peers was seemingly justified.

Ed's concept of heroism was shattered as he read the title of the course, "Heroism vs. Violence." Rather than blend these two traits into one entity of self-complacency, the title suggested that they were not united. For the first time Ed mentally teetered in acknowledging that *versus* implies opposites.

Here is where Jiminy Cricket, symbol of honesty, enters the scene. He becomes embedded within Ed's conscience, an integral part of honesty. Jiminy's prodding just won't let up from causing Ed's mind to conjure up an honest appraisal of his past and possibly continued actions. Ed found that the "conscience thing," with its thrust of honesty, displaced the need for acceptance by peers to display threatening or violent behavior. He then realized that just as he had believed he had power to please his peers while taunting others, he could also direct his negative inner strength into a stronger self-belief. He then called on that power to honestly acknowledge within himself that heroism and violence are actually at opposite poles in human behavior. The challenge of choice suddenly became an option to use the strength of this newfound value. It would actually be more courageous to not accept the bribes to cause havoc in the lives of others and still be even more courageous to use this inner strength of self-belief to foster positive values and actions within his daily routine.

In sharing such thoughts about courage with children/students, the intent is to guide them to make the more difficult choices in not agreeing to harmful and violent behavior as well as not being enticed into harming themselves by partaking in the drug/alcohol scene. Indeed, honesty in judging their motives in making their choices and following through with the courage of self-belief will lead back to the undaunted title of "Heroism vs. Violence."

Note Page

Like Ed in this article, how much do you think the emotional impact of being a hero leads to involvement in gangs in the second paragraph?

Please write your thoughts on this note page.

Do you think it is possible to share the concept of *conscience* as related to Jiminy Cricket, and how it can preserve the safekeeping of the inside nurturing of your children?

What are your thoughts on this all-important message?

Please write them below.

Propositional Preposition

Outside
Communicating "To," "At," Rules

Inside
Acceptance
"With," Sharings, Joys, Achievements

A Propositional Preposition

How many readers remember the lengthy list of prepositions that had to be memorized in middle-grade classrooms? These challenging words had to be committed to memory to be mentally available for use in well-structured and grammatically enhanced written assignments.

I have recently become aware that the preposition *with* presents a proposition to those whose lives are involved with children/students in whatever capacity.

According to Funk and Wagnall's dictionary, a proposition is, "a proposal offered for consideration." Indeed, *with* does offer a proposal for effectual and meaningful communication with our children/students. This proposal offers the insight to replace communicating "at" or "to" our children to "with" our children within their families.

"With" implies "not alone," a togetherness of some degree in exchanging thoughts, cares, concerns, joys, pains, fears, achievements, etc. It is like the yellow lines on the highway. Both sides of traffic can be seen and noticed. The contents of the cars can be viewed in slower traffic while at the same time respecting the boundary line of the other side.

Unlike the two-lane highway of "with," "to" and "at" form a one-way line. Cars are lined up in back of each other each limited to one view. "To" and "at" communications with our children involve directions, reminders, boundaries, responsibilities, consequences, rules, regulations, etc. These communications come from the established authority in the home.

Reading lends itself to both types of "propositional" communications. Often heard in the past and perhaps in the present are the following communications: "What a nice story; read it to me." "Jump into bed; I'll read to you." "Did you finish your book report?" "Read me your essay." Both participants are traveling on a one-way street of "to," each on their own road.

Now let us substitute "with" in the above scenarios. "You read that story nicely." "Here is what I think of this or that character." "It was fun reading that story together." "Thank you for sharing the book with me." "Your book report was great." "How do you feel about the ending?"

Quite obviously, we now have the two-lane highway. Both lanes are seen as well as heard from in response to each other. There is no right or wrong direction given "to" or "at" the child/student. Indeed, the inside of the persons communicating "with" each other makes for an enjoyable ride. They become important to each other and recognized within that status by each other. Neither one is traveling in the one-way line of isolation.

We need to make the effort to understand that just as crawling and gradual standing allow the baby's legs to attain the strength to walk, so the nurturing of our children's minds through our sharing with them will likewise strengthen them in leading them to make healthy and appropriate choices in challenging situations. This, in turn, will produce a healthy self-belief within themselves.

Focusing
Acceptance

Acceptance plays a large role in directing us toward our futures. We get acceptance letters from college deans, acknowledging that we are eligible to be enrolled in a college level of studies. A job application is read by a prospective employer, who informs us that our application was reviewed and we are accepted for the job or position we hoped to acquire. Our athletic ability is recognized by sports' scouting personnel, and we sign a contract in acceptance of the recognition of our ability to play the sport.

Impressions of our various abilities in the above scenarios as well as many others allow us to inwardly believe that we have been accepted as a person of value. When we experience the fact that we are a person of value by others, we become aware that we must be a person of value unto ourselves.

Such is the case when reading to/with our children. This can so impress upon them their importance in the eyes of the adult and can deeply show them that they are a valued member of the family.

The college dean, the employer, and the athletic scout are figures of authority giving a valued recognition to the personhood of the subject of the respective applications. Such is the case when a parent, and likewise an authority figure, recognizes the personhood of children and offers to share a few minutes of reading time with them. The seed of acceptance through personal affirmation by way of a parent's invitation to read together is sown and nurtured. Whether time is spent in reading about Spot, Puff, and Baby Sally, Harry Potter's next venture, a scientific discovery, or any other reading assignment from whatever grade level respective to the child, the togetherness in the world of sharing what was read with comments from each other will lead the child to discover another world. It is the child's world, where he is or she is experiencing the same excitement in being discovered within his home and eventually within himself.

Isolation leads to loneliness, depression, and possibly tragedy. Acceptance leads to an affirmation of self-belief and the inner motivation to repeat positive, healthy patterns of behavior toward the goals of success and happiness.

Note Page

Can you distinguish between outside nurturing and inside nurturing within the fourth and fifth paragraphs of this chapter? Write down your thoughts on this note page.

How will the inside nurturing help to produce a healthy self-belief within your children as read in the last paragraph?

Present your understanding of this concept on this note page.

Stop Thief

Outside
Movies, Tapes, Lyrics, Drugs,
Alcohol, Nicotine

Inside
Values
Time, Self-Respect, Willpower,
Family Inclusion

Stop, Thief!

It was earlier than usual that morning when Jake arrived at his gas station. He wanted to have all of the pumps in good working order. It would soon be time for the descent of traffic from the winter skiing crowd as they began an early trek home from their vacation treat. He turned the corner and approached the door. He was stunned as a black-clothed, ski-masked figure erupted from the doorway and fled with the speed of a downhill skier. Assuming the obvious, he yelled, "Stop, thief!" and entered his business to find his fears realized. He had been robbed.

Returning to the opened door, he saw the getaway car too far off in the distance to hope to catch the thief or vehicle. After reporting the theft to local authorities, he began a careful inspection of his losses. Some of his specialized tools were gone. These would be a great loss to him. His station was one of only a few in the area that could unravel the intricate mysteries within a car's working system. He had worked long, exhausting hours to protect and keep these tools in guarded and operating condition. He had felt secure in meeting the challenges within his life's profession. He decided to inspect the lock on the door, which had been jimmied to allow the intruder to enter. He found it uncomfortable to admit that he had intended to spend an extra half hour after closing to change that lock or add a deadbolt device, giving added protection to his inventory. He now realized if he had spent a little more time, even in his exhausted state at the end of the day, or in between serving customers, he might have followed through with his plan to give the tools and goods within his station stronger security.

Valued possessions such as home, car, jewelry, video equipment, etc., can often be replaced or restored through investing in insurance policies. Deadbolt locks, antitheft protectors, TV security via cable cameras, and hired security services are great tools in safeguarding our worldly possessions.

Within our children we find that there are no visible batteries, wires, or plugs that warn us that they are running out of energy, as might be the case with Jake's tools. The battery that empowers our children's lives is within them, in their spirits—that unseen but very real entity within their personhood. This spirit, as it follows each stage of development, surely needs security measures of protection lest, like Jake, we suddenly need to shout, "Stop, thief!"

Movies, tapes, lyrics, TV programs, fashions, violence, language, weapons, toys of violent nature, food choices, commercials, speeding car ads that silently invite our young drivers to do likewise, nicotine, alcohol, and drugs are daily masked thieves such as entered Jake's workplace.

The audio and visual offerings rob our children and young people of the joy that was within them as younger children. The childhood lyrics, films, and stories presented a picture of positive excitement and happy outcomes. These same mediums of entertainment now project violence, cruelty, harshness, and weaponry in the guise of heroic actions. Again, we need to yell, "Stop, thief!" and carefully choose our entertainment within our homes and share the meaning and value of self-respect by way of choices that bear witness to our concerns.

Commercials of images of cars going at great speeds and often in circular motions entertain the vulnerable minds and imaginations of our teens that they can do likewise. The only difference is that our young people die in a crash and the ads continue their luring excitement on the screen. They need to hear the call, "Stop, thief," as they rob these young people of respect within a vehicle as well as the willpower to follow the safety regulations of safe driving.

Nicotine, drugs, and alcohol, so often viewed as the acceptance test of peer belonging, need to hear a loud and clear, "Stop, thief," as these addictions rob our young people of the self-respect they had as young children. Once this level of worthlessness is reached, the very heroes of nicotine, alcohol, and drugs become the greatest thieves of all, the takers of human lives.

It is possible to figuratively add a lock or deadbolt device, as Jake might have done to his tool inventory, to our highly invested human inventory, our children. The antitheft device can turn into a table at which each member of the family can share one thought about what respect means to them. Perhaps most can meet at a given selected time. (Respect.)

A preschool youngster can be guided into sharing about what happens on the inside after making a good choice. (Joy, happiness.)

Early elementary children can be introduced to the term *consequences*. How do we avoid an unhealthy or painful consequence? (Will power, self-respect, obedience.)

Upper elementary children can be asked, "How does it feel to have assignments done neatly and handed in on time?" (Pride in work, responsibility, accountability.)

Middle school students can be asked, "Which is more difficult to say, yes to an inappropriate suggestion or No, I'd rather not and walk away?" (Strong self-belief, courage.)

High school children can be asked, "What kind of inner consequences are felt from the following choices: completed assignments, test preparedness, involvement in school activities, respect for peers, saying no to inappropriate suggestions?" (Self-pride, self-respect, self-responsibility.)

Happiness, joy, self-respect, personal pride, self-belief, self-responsibility, and self- affirmation are all inner affirmations found within and around the family table. Indeed, in following Jake's example, the above-mentioned descriptions are very strong antitheft values safeguarding the inner spirits of our children. If nurtured within our children of age and grades levels, inherent vices presented and projected toward our children will find a stalwart security system within our families.

Focusing
Values

A value is an asset, a favorable component in various aspects in life as well as in human behavior. The assets of favorable business investments lead to an indicated growth in the economy. Good health is an asset as it allows us to partake in various activities, such as sports, traveling, jogging, recreational ventures, etc. Home ownership is an asset that allows us to be mortgage free and also allows us the availability of personal financial savings. Our cars are assets giving us the privilege to drive to almost any reasonable destination. Jake's tools were assets to him as they promoted growth and accuracy in his business.

There is a most pertinent question to be asked within the context of assets. Why is less attention and concern given to the assets affecting human behavior? Why is so much attention given to the things we do and less attention to who we are and how we live? In dealing with children, we need to look within ourselves and try to find evidence of very special assets called values. This materialistic world needs our commitment to introduce and nurture, in sharing by example, that personal values of happiness and self-affirmation are inner assets. We need to guide them in understanding that they are safeguards in protecting us against the insidious thievery found in today's most questionable entertainment genres. The lives of children/young adults are surrounded by the seductive lures of motion pictures, TV movies, and video games. The depiction of scenes of lurid sex, graphic nudity, horrific violence of video games, and the crudeness of offensive language degrading family values in animated movies and TV programs indeed rob our children of the sense of values to be found in respect, honesty, self-belief, and others mentioned in this article, which alone can show them happy and self-respectable lives.

Another thief of values lurks within the toy industry's sensational figures and weapons, all in the name of heroes to be admired and imitated. Three-year-olds are now absorbing the message that violence and fighting are the only ways to solve problems or to react to the challenging behavior of a peer or sibling. Indeed, these violent gestures in the name of family entertainment are robbing our young people of self-respect and need to hear the call, "Stop, thief!"

Jake was stunned as he encountered the obvious physical evidence of the thief emerging from his garage where his assets and tools were kept. Parallel to this scene, adults are often stunned by the unexpected actions of young people. Jake sadly admitted that he had not done enough to ensure the safety of his tools because he did not find enough time to protect his assets.

Unlike Jake, who only lost things, adults can help children discover the human assets of family values through practicing together the list of honorable traits found at the end of the article, "Stop, Thief." As Jake needed a more durable lock for his garage's valuables, so the family can install the strong inner lock of affirmation and self-belief within children and possibly may never have to arrive at a sudden shock in behavior and join Jake in yelling within themselves, "Stop, thief."

Note Page

What is your response to the last paragraph of the chapter? Do you agree that it holds the solution to the thieves of values in today's society?

Write your answer on this note page.

Go back to the list of ideas for help on the above question. Which ones could be introduced into your family?

Present your thoughts on this note page.

To Be or Not to Be

Outside
Actions, Popularity, Blame

Inside
Choices
To Be, Inner Strength, Praise,
Self-Belief, Individuality

To Be or Not to Be

I find myself wondering if Bill the Bard would ever know how appropriate some titles of his plays are today and how important a message they still carry hundreds of years after Hamlet left the stage.

"To be or not to be," Hamlet's famous soliloquy, can give us cause to consider what life is or will be about in the lives of our children. It is actually a question silently asked as parents view their newborn infants with future visions of the child presented momentarily in each stage of life.

"To be" can imply a healthy self-image built from the continual familial nurturing of the inner spirit. It is an inner neon sign that portrays a healthy, trusting self-belief through which healthy choices can be made in challenging situations.

A car cannot go where we want it to go unless there is gas inside the engine. A toy won't move by itself unless the inner spring is wound. The sailboat won't float downstream unless the natural current beneath it moves it downstream.

The ability to make healthy, appropriate choices stems from the natural current of willpower, which results in the answer to Hamlet's question, "To be."

In contrast, the second half of Hamlet's question, "Or not to be," has been sorrowfully evidenced clear across our country and at times, in our own neighborhoods. We have viewed and families have lived the tragic consequences of violent behavior. When this happens, surely the inner spirit, that neon sign of "to be," was not illuminated with personal inner strength to believe in its own validity.

Where is a discrepancy between a student's belief that he can drive a car and the belief that he can say no to an inappropriate or unacceptable situation? Driving a car means having an outer strength to maneuver a vehicle. Being unable to say no to negative behavior stems from children questioning their inner beliefs about who they are as people. They are all stored in the same place—inside the vehicle., inside the nurtured self belief.

Being displeased with her young daughter's playing with the silverware at a nearby restaurant, the parent addressed the child with harsh, judgmental words: "You bad, bad girl." A small child's brain is not yet developed to the point of making a distinction between unacceptable behavior and the one whose behavior is unacceptable. Children of many ages tend to think, *I am what I do.*

Children often see themselves as a result of an adult's judgment of their actions. We as adults witness and remember the good times, the happy smiles as they receive affirmation for a job well done. At times, we seem unaware of the presence of rejection when we penetrate the same inner space with a negative reaction, which turns affirmation into self-blame and can set the stage for "to be" being replaced with "not to be."

Early childhood years lend themselves to molding minds toward strong wills. I do not refer to the strong will that wants what it wants at this early age. Rather, I mean early efforts in practicing to choose healthy choices and thus rewarding them with a strong "to be." This will strengthen their paths within each new day. As was witnessed in a preschool classroom, we should say things like, "Billy, that was very nice of you to choose to share your toy with Susan. "I am proud of you."

Elementary school–age children's sense of "to be" is formed by the emergence of countless choices found within their daily routine in the school environment. Being in the position of captain to choose his teammates at recess, Ed chooses a less-proficient student in the line-up who is often picked last. Choosing people in spite of their lack of popularity will help to establish a strong personal strength of "to be."

The middle school student's sense of "to be" rests on self-attained evidence that he needs only a strong belief in his own personhood and should not be available to the lures and dares of his peers. We can affirm this with statements like, "I was impressed with the way you chose not to take the cigarette from your classmate. Your strong sense of belief in yourself was evident when you turned and walked away."

The high school student has the prerogative to stand on the strength of a certain amount of maturity reached at this level. Receiving affirmation at home and school, sharing opinions, exchanging thoughts, receiving respectful acknowledgments of his individuality, and having well-defined, guided boundaries will foster further growth in attaining the authentic "to be."

The spirit of William Shakespeare has shared modern insights. What message could other play titles have for us? Let us not look back on the childhood and schooldays of our children and find that we had a "comedy of errors." May our "love's labor" never be lost. May our dreams for our children never be limited to "a midsummer's night."

Finally, in lovingly helping our children attain a healthy self-image within their own personhoods "to be" and continuing to guide them away from choices that cause them "not to be," we can joyously revel in the thought that in their and our futures, "all's well that ends well."

Focusing
Choices

A well-written assignment in English class was to include the five Ws: Who? What? When? Where? Why? Structuring our thoughts and sentences around the answers to these interrogative pronouns allowed the writer to see where his story was headed. There was an expectant hope to receive a well-deserved A on his paper.

"To be" implies life, living life, and living with the daily answers to the five W's as they spontaneously occur each day. The answers to these questions cannot be reached without making choices, sometimes thoughtfully arrived at but often made at a moment of a pressured challenge from another. These choices involve mentally and often emotionally carrying on a conversation with oneself. Whom should I ask? What do I do? Why should I do what I really don't want to do? Where will it take me? When do I meet you?

The choices made while considering the answers to similar questions must be dealt with also from within our children/students. The concept of "to be" is fulfilled in our children's lives when strong, courageous choices are made from the inner strength of family nurturing. Self-respect, self- belief, and affirmation of being a valued family member through involvement in family life and decisions will serve to offset the consequences that follow a harmful choice that may result in blame rather than praise. Hence the concept of "to be" may be the route chosen and eventually supplant the positive values that lead to a happy, well-adjusted life.

In closing, I would suggest that readers highlight concepts within this chapter that spark parental recognition of the emotional needs of our children/students. Such acknowledgment may result in the strengthening of making the appropriate choice, resulting in "to be" rather than "not to be." As our young children reach the status of young adulthood, we can therefore agree with the English poet that within our family life, "all's well that ends well."

Note Page

Having read the entire chapter, can you relate to the message in the sixth paragraph?

Share your feelings on this note page.

Have there been instances in your home where the scenes described in the chapter have possibly been experienced in the part you cannot see within your children?

Are you gathering insights into the effects of such episodes?

Tell yourself about them on this note page.

Marketing Strategy
"Polishing The Product"

Outside
Obesity, Peer Pressure, Aloneness

Inside
Affirmation
Praise, Recognition, "I Believe,"
Opinions, Trust

A Marketing Strategy
Polishing the Product

Marketing 101

Course Description: This course will give the student the opportunity to view different marketing strategies. Stress will be placed not only on the outer appearance of the product but also on the inner quality within the essence of the item.

The above hypothetical course came to my mind as I was reading the comments about Walter Peyton, a distinguished and honorable hero in the football arena. In the Sports section of *USA Today* (11/9/99), the article alluded to the belief that Walter Peyton was a model person before he accomplished his marvelous rushing record. All his goodness started in his family. When he arrived at JSU he was polished already.

How applicable these comments are to the course description of Marketing 101. We read how Walter Peyton was indeed polished outwardly in his uncanny ability to play football, and apparently the "polishing" was not lost on his coaches or teammates. Indeed, as is indicated and believed, the "polishing" was accomplished by his family throughout his lifetime.

Actually, if we stop long enough to think about it for a moment, we do use a portion of our time in doing some polishing. We polish furniture, silverware, cars, and other items when we want them to look nice to others and more importantly to ourselves. However, in our haste to use our scarcity of time, we are apt to overlook the polishing of the most important product in our lives and in our households: our *children*. Of course, the polishing does not take the form of the swish of a duster or a spray of Pledge, both of which add sheen to the outer surface. With our children the polishing needs to be done to the inside, the part we cannot see.

There are children of all ages and all grade levels who I believing are lacking this inner polishing. They are often left out of school activities. They become the last one picked or are not picked for a kickball team or other sport at recess. They are often the ones who sit alone in the cafeteria with little self-belief to sit with others. They are the ones who get few phone calls from classmates and who walk home alone. They are the ones who are given judgmental looks from their peers about the way they dress, wearing controversial accessories or outdated clothes, or perhaps they present an obese image that turns heads the other way. Therefore, they walk alone. Perhaps the inner polish is missing in their lives in spite of their outward appearance of stylish clothes or hairstyles.

We need to patent a polishing cloth that can reach into the abandoned aloneness of these children/ students. It is often too late when others of the same unpolished nature band together in a destructive group or pair their identity to society or school populations with violent weaponry, as seen across the country. They spew out their anger and loneliness because they haven't been able to secure within themselves their ability to trust the confidence of another. The "polishing" has been rejected, and it soon follows that little affirmation yields little conformity.

Rather than wait with expectancy that somewhere along the line the request to be heard or listened to will be made by our children, it is up to us, the adults, to extend that invitation. Shared opinions, shared time of ten to fifteen minutes, and shared discussions are offers that can come from us. If I ask a child, "How was your day?" and he answers, "Fine" and the conversation ends, that is a sample of communication, but it is not a sharing experience. I need to continue and say, "My day was very busy, and I would like to share it with you." I am then inviting the child into my world.

It is my opinion that we need to introduce this sharing technique into our family units at an early age, possibly around the third or fourth grade, if not sooner. Allow me to offer a few strategies for polishing the outer layer of our children.

1. I'll ask you the third table and you can ask me the sixth. (ten min.)
2. I'll ask you half of your spelling list, and you can ask me the other half. (ten min.)
3. Let's read a story in your reader, reading every other paragraph. Which character did you like the best? I'll tell you mine. (fifteen min.)
4. I'll ask you the first six states and their capitals on your list. Let's review them together first. (fifteen min.)
5. In five minutes, how many nouns can you write down just from the kitchen area? (ten min.)
6. In your opinion, what does making a healthy choice mean to you? Let me share what it means to me . (twenty min.)
7. Do we have to say "yes" when someone suggests an inappropriate choice? Why do you think it would be inappropriate? (twenty min.)
8. Let's each write six or seven lines sharing how we think it would be to be the last leaf on a tree in late fall. What feelings would we share? (twenty min.)
9. Let's each of us share our opinion about homework. (twenty min.)
10. Let's tell each other how we feel about this special time we have shared with each other. (twenty to twenty-five min.)

This list can go on and on. Can you see how the sharing comes from the space or inner area that is hidden by the clothes and sometimes difficult to find behind the jewelry or makeup? I believe it is also difficult for children/students within themselves. They need us to guide them to its existence and nurture the continued self-awareness brought out by our affirming that they are valued enough to share our time.

If you can manage these short intervals of time a few times a week among your children and among the vast responsibilities within your household, you soon will wear out your polishing cloth and most adequately fulfill the requirements of Marketing 101.

Focusing
Affirmation

How many of the following scenes are familiar? The infant takes his first steps toward Mom and Dad. Cheers, smiles, and clapping hands sprout forth from both parents. Baby's face lights up. He has successfully walked a wee distance. The smiles and outward glee are expressed by his parents and are absorbed by his inner senses of accomplishment as well as a happy sensation of affirming himself to himself, with himself. Hence, the happy reaction of his excited smile, uplifted hands, and happy gurgle.

Preschool, kindergarten, and primary grade level children react similarly when their schoolroom accomplishments are recognized by teachers and parents. In having pleased those in an authority role, the children/students often direct this pleasurable response of acceptance into their own inner existence. They have pleased those in adult roles; therefore they have reason to be pleased with themselves. Furthermore, they have been affirmed by adults and thus inwardly affirmed within themselves.

The process of recognizing the scholastic efforts and successes of our children follows every grade level, and many respond graciously to those affirmations and strive for repeated performances through each advanced grade level.

"Polishing the Product" reminds us of the deep needs of our children/students to be continually nurtured, or polished, by those who review their academic performance. However, we cannot limit our affirmations on what our children do in their lives. We also need to polish the inside, the emotional system with the affirmative polish of approval of who they are.

Times of praise and recognition need to be followed with, "I am proud of you." The smiles, claps, words, rewards, etc., remain on the outside, along with the recognition of whatever deed has been accomplished. "I am proud of *you*" directs itself to the inner polishing and focusing on the nurturing of the inner belief within our children. If they are led to a belief within themselves, then the recognition of such successes becomes the polish on their own self-image.

In discussing an upcoming test, the comment, "I know you can do it," can be changed to, "I believe you can do it." Coming from an adult, "I know" is an automatic preappraisal of his ability. Adults are supposed to know. However, "I believe" shifts the inner conviction of the adult directly into the inner conviction and deeply felt affirmation within the child/student. "I know" is an outside-to-outside acknowledgment. "I believe" is an inside-to-inside affirmation.

The chapter continues to remind us that the "I believe" strategy is deeply needed in the lives of children/students who rarely hear the congratulatory response of "nice work" and "good job" to their schoolwork. In reality, Bs, Cs, and Ds do not usually emit such recognition for work below the norm of acceptable grade level status. So many of these students live on the evidence of what they do or don't do. They often judge themselves in like manner. Unfortunately, their corresponding conclusion in their minds may be that they are also bad. The polishing cloth must be found and put to good use in such self-incriminating circumstances. It must guide the child/student to believe that he/she is a person and separate from the deed. It must affirm within them that they are still loved but only the deed or actions are unacceptable. This polishes the part we cannot see. This chapter offers suggested ways to polish our children/students beyond the outer layers of clothes, hairstyles, cosmetics, etc.

In the act of polishing (affirming) our children, there is an offered guarantee that like household spray polishes, it will leave our children with a lasting inner shine.

Note Page

How strong a message is the last paragraph regarding the part we cannot see within our children?

Write your thoughts on this note page.

How meaningful to you are the last two paragraphs as awarenesses in your parental nurturing of the part you cannot see within your children?

Offer a response on this note page.

Fitting Together the Pieces of the Academic Pie

The signs of spring are finally upon us. The crocuses are in bloom. The forsythia will soon be budding, and guess what else? Another round of MCAS challenges are upon us.

Unfortunately, much emphasis has been placed on the negative results of these tests. We have focused on the number of students whose low scores indicate a lack in calculating objective answers and in critical thinking skills as seen in the subjective requirements of the test. The reason for students' poor performances is sought out and remedied. In searching for the explanation for the seemingly unaccountable test performances of low-scoring students, we need to apply our considerations to the MCAS assessments that took place in the earlier lives of our students.

This test preparedness started with the take-home primer vocabulary words that accompanied the first-grade reader; the more challenging sight vocabulary words of grade two; the practice and repetition of math facts from grade three; the hearing of recitation of math tables from grade four; the memorization of states and capitals from grade five; the knowledge of other countries and lifestyles that share the same planet as the United States in grade six; the application and respect for grammar and punctuation in written assignments and homework in grade seven; and the personal, concentrated effort to turn in an assignment with an expressed opinion or a list of factual data that bespeaks a well-informed and self-believed mind in grade eight.

The concepts of the MCAS testing came as a shock to the three constituents within our educational system: parents, teachers, and students. Our students have been expected to give witness to their current abilities at the time of the testing. Those students who established a pattern of parental involvement and successful teaching methods and assessments, accompanied by an educational attitude, attentiveness, and effort, passed the MCAS testing or at least placed only a short distance away from passing the expected norm. It is unrealistic to expect personal scholastic accountability to be suddenly established on a higher grade level if it has been absent during earlier elementary years.

The MCAS tests have gone through much scrutiny and revision, as have many teaching methods since their original conception. Scenes have changed in classrooms. Voices are heard by way of expressing opinions in addition to reciting assigned data. Critical thinking skills are being nurtured and strengthened instead of doing worksheet papers or listening to a teacher's instructional presentation with little input from students.

Many students have absorbed the shock and stress of these tests and are presently dealing with the accountability awareness necessary for scholastic success.

The last third of the scholastic pie still needs to be strengthened by initiating home involvement in the education of our students. Actually, it is this sector that has the greater challenge for such involvement by parents because of busy work schedules combined with home responsibilities. These two factors leave little time for family members to connect with one another.

In so many instances, school has become only a responsibility. This happens with no surprise when there is little sharing in the world of learning on all grade levels. The sad outcome of this situation is that a negative, unsuccessful pattern continues throughout the grade levels. I believe that the result is not, for many, due to lack of intelligence. It is due to expectations put on some students to carry the full responsibility for academic achievement all by themselves. This can be nearly impossible when they are living in academic isolation.

Congratulations and well wishes to those whose academic pie has had three consistent pieces evident in their daily scholastic lives. Three is not a crowd where education, happiness, well-being, and success are concerned. Teachers, parents, and students are all responsible for the successful acquisition of knowledge at all grade levels.

Let us learn a lesson from the painful experiences of past MCAS scores. Perhaps a concentrated effort can be made to nurture the growth of academic skills during the elementary grades. This effort, in turn, may become the bridge to MCAS success in middle school and high school.

With the symbol of the educational pie in mind, perhaps our families, classrooms, neighborhoods, and cities will reap the benefits of happy, self-affirmed, successful young people.

Focusing
Education

The ritual for the established entrance into the academic world historically continues each year. Having reached the age of five years, preschool is left behind. August heralds in the fall collection of back-to-school fashions, and the kindergarten inductee is included in this shopping frenzy. From head to toe tiers of impressionable styles adorn the littlest angel, igniting a sense of excitement of waiting for the school bus as well as within the parental expectations of early academic success. This established routine repeats itself in the fall of every year as every grade level, kindergarten through college, returns to the challenge of the books.

But why do we take so much mall-walking time, window shopping, and stretching of budgets to ensure ourselves and our children that the outer appearance will prompt success when it is the inside of each student that will produce success as well as happiness? Furthermore, how much of this inside have we nurtured within our children/students so they can believe in it and rely on it at the many challenging moments in their scholastic lives? Have we adorned the inside of our children/students with a strong sense of self-belief throughout at least momentary pauses to exchange with them how five minutes of our day was spent and perhaps how we dealt with a challenge on our own level? Have we extended this invitation to our children/students, ensuring them that we are interested in their day—not just checking on them but from a sincere effort to personally share our respective days with them? Our children need to know that we also have challenges at home and within the work world and most especially that we also do not like what we have to do at any given time but that we know things must be done in spite of how we feel about doing them.

Have we found a few minutes of time to discuss the concept of values with them? The simplest chat about being happy because our younger children were polite as well as feeling a warm sense of pride to the more in-depth discussion of accountability as lived in the lives of our older students relative to class assignments, etc., are ways of meaningfully communicating.

No matter how dazzling the outside of our children/students appears, their inner core must emit from within them to themselves a strong self-belief that they do not have to give in to unhealthy enticements that infringe upon their own value systems.

The bridge of parental communications reaching into the world of children/students as a simple sharing of each other's world should undoubtedly foster as well as nurture them. Along with shared values of respect, kindness, toleration, and responsibility, they can then see themselves as intrinsic values within their families.

Note Page

Which piece of the academic pie as described throughout the article is most meaningful to you? Can you apply it to your children within your family involvement?

Share your thoughts on this note page.

How does accountability fit into the last paragraph?

Write your response on this note page.

A Final Focusing

(Parental)
Inside
Openness of Mind, Patience, Affirming, Personhood

A Final Focusing
"Understanding"

I sincerely hope that some instances of enlightenment found meaning within you to continue to foster your wish for happiness and success within the lives of your children.

Together we have acknowledged the physical presence of our five senses, their operative organs within our bodies, and their respective reactions to the stimuli of sight, sound, touch, hearing, and taste.

Throughout these articles we have also shared and acknowledged the presence of invisible senses within each of us and our children that direct all of us toward happiness and successful lives. Choices, attitudes, decisions, affirmations, self-confidence, self-belief, etc., accompanied by the focusing values in these chapters will provide the means of realizing and bringing to fruition authentic and validated members of a family unit.

Understanding implies an openness of mind, making our love and acceptance available toward the actions and reactions of our children. Understanding allows us to plant the seed of affirmation within our children, as children often see themselves as mirrored from the adult's acceptance of who they are as a valuable member of the family unit.

In closing, I respect you as you accept the challenges you meet within the responsibilities of your family. I honor you as you live in understanding the willingness within yourselves in loving, honoring, respecting, and nurturing the personhoods within each of your children.

—Margaret Redfern, author

Note Page

Reread the fourth paragraph. How does the second sentence apply to you within the nurturing of your children as a parent?

Express your thoughts on this note page.

What are your thoughts on how you can live out the concepts offered in the final paragraph?

Parenthood
A Child's Expectations

Preparing me to live a happy life.
Asking me how I spent my day.
Reaching into my world of school.
Enabling me to be happy about myself.
Noticing me as a person.
Talking with me about my world and my feelings.
Hearing my *inside story*.
Offering a listening ear.
Overcoming immediate judgments.
Dispense praise; dilute blame.

Child's inner affirmation: Your love as shown above will be inside of me to use whenever I need it in making healthy choices

Parenthood
(A Child's Expectations)

(A poetic summary of the book.)

Try to read the lines from within your own inside.

The first letter of each line spells "parenthood."

Have your children read to you the affirmation below the poem.

What does the poem and its contents mean to you? Do you have a better understanding of parental nurturing?

Further comments, communications can be sent to me via my e-mail address: Uzzie36@aol.com

Final Reviews

What's inside the Wrapper?

OUTSIDE

Homework, Chores, Sports, Robot

The package is a child predisposed to our care and guidance with responsibility on his or her part to honor and obey our tenets. This includes homework, chores, being ready to go where and when we need to go, and listening to and performing our dos and don'ts.

INSIDE

Valued Opinions, "I-Ness," Personhood

A daily sharing in and receiving of what our children offer is nurturing them through their own inner giving, resulting in positive growth patterns. Thus, inside the wrapper of the child's personhood will be an established affirmation that he is a valuable asset to life as lived by himself and among his peers.

Outside vs. Inside

OUTSIDE

Eyes, Ears, Nose, Throat, Taste

We always care for the outside of the body. The five senses are parts of the outsides of our bodies.

INSIDE

Unseen Parts, Personhood, Discovery

The essence of my sharing is that I believe we must continue to make a gallant effort to reach the inside, the place or space within our children where an affirmation of them as people will forever need nurturing most, especially within their academic journey.

Why Don't Our Flowers Blossom?

OUTSIDE

Peer Pressure, Complacency, Exclusion

I didn't remember to tend the root with preventative measures against the invading pressures that would stunt its growth or destroy the essence of its being.

INSIDE

Nurturing

In the garden of human beings, there is no difference between the deep need for *time* spent with them during these years when their roots are following the beckoning of unknown challenges.

Heroism vs. Violence

OUTSIDE

Peer Hero, Bravado, Image, Daring

His spirit was being nurtured by the recognition of his peers as they responded to his actions with smiles, applause, and invitations to join the group.

INSIDE

Courage, Choices, Conscience, Self-Belief

He could almost visualize Jiminy's eyes staring right into his ego as the recognition of his unrighteous actions was being judged.

A Propositional Preposition

OUTSIDE

Communicating "To," "At," Rules, Boundaries, Responsibilities

"To" and "At" communications with our children involve directions, reminders, boundaries, responsibilities, consequences, rules, regulations, etc. These communications come from the established authority in the home.

INSIDE

Acceptance

"With," Sharings, Joys, Achievements

"With" implies "not alone," a togetherness of some degree in exchanging thoughts, cares, concerns, joys, pains, fears, achievements, etc.

Stop, Thief

OUTSIDE

Movies, Tapes, Lyrics, Drugs, Alcohol, Nicotine

Once this level of worthlessness is reached, the very heroes of nicotine, alcohol and drugs become the greatest thieves of all, the takers of human lives.

INSIDE

Values

Happiness, joy, self-respect, personal pride, self-belief, self-responsibility, and self-affirmation are very strong antitheft values safeguarding the inner spirits of our children.

To Be or Not To Be

OUTSIDE

Actions, Popularity, Blame

Surely that inner spirit, that neon sign of "to be," was not illuminated with its own personal strength to believe in its own validity.

INSIDE

Choices

"To Be," Inner Strength, Praise, Self-Belief, Individuality

"To be" can imply a healthy self-image built from the continual familial nurturing of the inner spirit. It is an inner neon sign that portrays a healthy, trusting self-belief through which appropriate choices can be made in challenging situations.

A Marketing Strategy

Polishing the Product

OUTSIDE

Unpolished, Loneliness, Unaccepted

We need to patent a polishing cloth that can reach into the abandoned aloneness of these children/students. The polishing has been rejected, and it soon follows that little affirmation yields little conformity.

INSIDE

Within-ness, Polishing Cloth, Affirmation

Actually, if we stop long enough to think about it for a moment, we do use a portion of our time to do some polishing. Of course, the polishing does not take the form of a swish with a duster or a spray of Pledge, both of which will add sheen to the outer surface. With our children, the polishing needs to be done to the inside, the "within-ness" of each child.

Margaret Redfern's verse from her book, "A Child's Expectations",
epitomizes the Child in Everywhere in the world in which we live.
The quoted line at the end of the verse indicates affirmation of the reached
expectations offered throughout the pages of this inspired book.

About the Author

Margaret Redfern is a teacher who writes from both her head and her heart. Her writings come forth from her spirit/soul. Her head tells her what each student can do, while her heart tells her who they are within their personhoods.

Her writings come forth in what she has written on behalf of recognizing the inside of children within her classrooms. Parental inner nurturing -self-belief, acceptance, personhood, values, choices, affirmation and understanding are often not found within parental care as parents are often overwhelmed by a multitude of parental responsibilities simply to feed, clothe and shelter children along with time consuming sport activities. Her poem, "A Child's Expectations" is written in the voice of a child.

Years later in retirement the following words were said to her by a former student: "You will be with me until the day I die." Enough said!

Books:

Christmas Crib Angel (A book about hope in Christmas loss, especially for children.)

Thaddeus Centipede Needs New Shoes (He actually does find one hundred of them!)

Maddie's Magic Tree (Maddie watches the magic tree and animals as the tree performs its magic!)

Tel: 781-665-4796 • E-mail: uzzie36@aol.com
49 Melrose Street, 6F, Melrose, Massachusetts, 02176

Printed in the United States
By Bookmasters